INVENTORY 98

INVENTORY 1985

## Books by Ogden Nash

I'm a Stranger Here Myself
Good Intentions
Many Long Years Ago
Versus
Family Reunion
The Private Dining Room and Other New Verses
You Can't Get There from Here
Verses from 1929 On (*selections from published works*)
Everyone but Thee and Me
Marriage Lines: Notes of a Student Husband
Santa Go Home

*For Young Readers:*

Parents Keep Out: Elderly Poems for Youngerly Readers
The Christmas That Almost Wasn't
Custard the Dragon
Custard the Dragon and the Wicked Knight
The New Nutcracker Suite and Other Innocent Verses
The Adventures of Isabel
The Untold Adventures of Santa Claus

# Santa Go Home

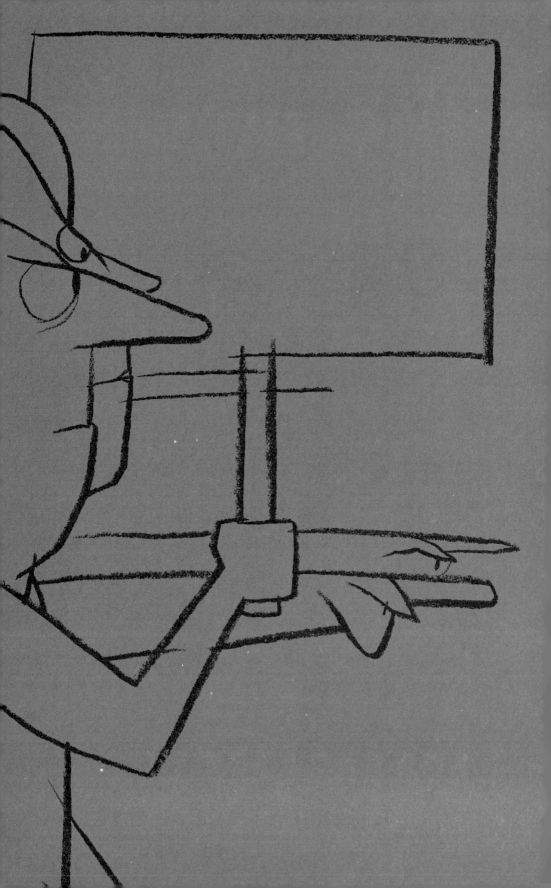

# Santa Go Home

## A Case History for Parents

### by OGDEN NASH

embellished by
ROBERT OSBORN

Little, Brown and Company • Boston • Toronto

# Foreword

These lines of prose are written by a freak with a knack for rudimentary versification. The freakishness and the knack have enabled me to be my own master for nearly thirty-five years, with certain qualifications. To be specific, as a journeyman rhymer I am frequently called upon by editors to supply them with seasonal material. Seasonal material is another term for Christmas verses. I suppose that I have written some fifty Christmas verses by now, which means having come up with fifty different approaches to, or treatments of, the theme.

Last year I felt that my Noëling days were over; that I had caterwauled the last carol, exploded the last ho-ho!; squeezed the last drop of brandy from the last raisin in the pudding. I therefore let it be known that I was no longer available for the annual Christmas chore. Odes to Mother's Day, Valentine's Day, April Fool's Day, National Apple Week, yes, but Christmas, nevermore. Santa Claus, that Old Man of the Season, was off my back. Since all Christmas verses are written in June or July, my thoughts were free to turn to the beach (live) and baseball (TV).

Then came an invitation from a respected editor which I could not refuse. He asked me to do a piece exploring the dark and hitherto hidden phases of the childhood of Santa Claus as revealed by the searchlight of modern child psychology; in short, to seek out and expose the influences and experiences, psychotic and traumatic, that gradually transformed a run of the shish kebab brat of Asia Minor into the full-grown monster known today to parents of the Western world. What hard-line Santaphobe could resist such a lure?

Eight volumes amounting to some twenty pounds of books on child psychology arrived the next day, and I descended eagerly into the jargon basement. Three weeks of poking and prying, pinching, weighing and pricing left me with the conviction that if I still could not love the beloved saint I could at least understand him. The following verse is the result of my studies.

When I had written the final line I presented, perhaps unwisely, the source books to the local library. If I have thereby set a time bomb ticking under the white clapboard houses of North Hampton, New Hampshire, retribution is only six or seven years away. Our beach may be infested with misunderstood siblings and frustrated Total Mother Persons, and I will find no refuge but the chimney, where on some Homeric Christmas Eve I shall at last confront my predestined foe. I cannot predict the outcome of the battle, but I presume that the victor will draw the body of the runner-up twenty times around the walls of F. A. O. Schwarz. Don't think of this as barbarism; every psychologist knows it's only Postfrustration Play.

OGDEN NASH

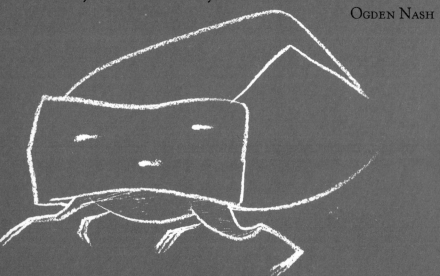

# Santa Go Home

My fellow parents,
The time has come
To realize that we've been dumb,
That century in
And century out
We have been hooked like silly trout,
That as our bank accounts have dwindled,
We have been hoodwinked,
Gypped, and swindled —
The victims of a confidence game
So blatant
We should blush with shame.
Who,
Though his banker eyes him dourly,
Doth crack his nest egg
Prematurely?
Who with the hungry loan shark battles
And pledges all his goods and chattels?

Who cons,
Until his vision fogs,
The endless Christmas catalogues?
Who crawls, exhausted,
On all fours
Through toyshops
And department stores?
Who burns the lonely midnight taper
In futile struggle
With wrapping paper,

Entangled fast
From toe to head
In writhing ribbons green and red?
Who toils
From Christmas Eve to Morn
The tree to lavishly adorn?
Who's taken months of loving care
To stuff those stockings hanging there?
Who, bedded at five,
At six doth rise,
Waked by impatient childish cries?
Who can this selfless mortal be?
I'll tell you who:
It's you and me.
Who gets the gratitude and applause?
I'll tell you who:

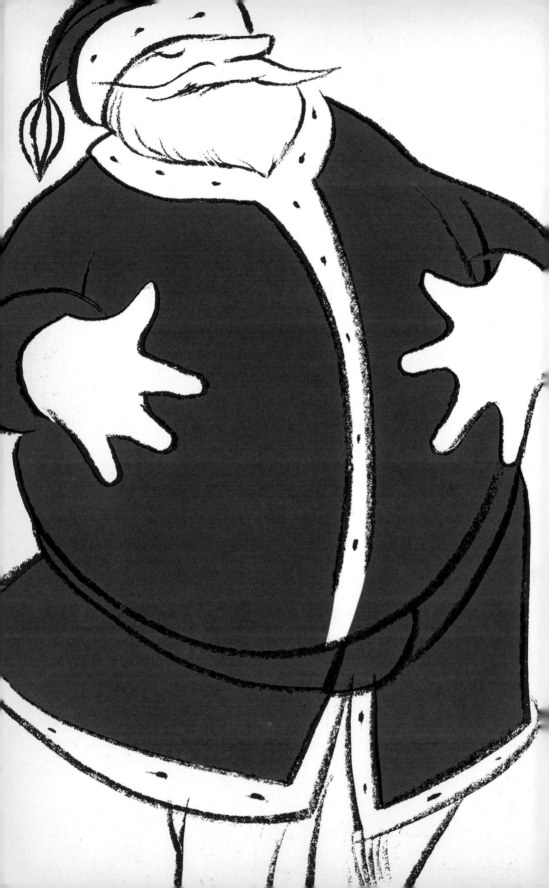

It's Santa Claus.

The reason I shall now discuss.
We worked backstage,
Anonymous,
But the recognition we renounced
To hands less scrupulous has bounced,
And been appropriated by
Kind Santa with the twinkling eye —

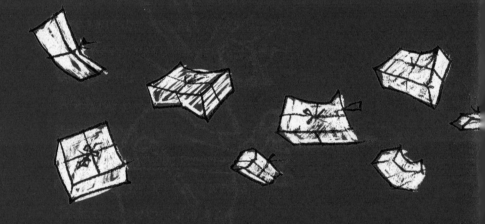

That genial,
Jolly,
Generous donor
Of gifts of which he's not the owner;

That carefree spendthrift,
Openhanded,
As sugary as an apple candied,
Distributing with pretended stealth
Somebody else's
Hard-earned wealth —
Who poses,
Like a strutting actor,
As the children's friend and benefactor.


Well, he can't be sued for his depredations —
He's absolved by the statute of limitations;
Too long ago
Our chance we foozled,
Allowing ourselves to be bamboozled.
Against his frauds we've no recourse.
But let us trace them to their source,
Investigate
The childhood home
Of this fat maladjusted gnome.

Let's analyze
His budding psychoses,
His traumas,
Tantrums,
And neuroses.
Let's probe the id,
Particu·larly,
Of this freeloading good·time Charlie.
And then perhaps we'll find the cause
Of why he grew up to be Santa Claus.
We'll trace his infancy round the clock
With sages such as Ilg and Spock.

His birth took place,
It's written down,
In Myra, an Asia Minor town.

This was,

As everyone must know,

Some sixteen centuries ago.

His childhood must have been disturbed,

The Autonomy of his Ego curbed;

He must have lacked,

In early years,

Emphatic Responses to his Peers.

He never got a mark of A

In Pre- or Postfrustration Play,

And, even as a

Neonatus,

Achieved no

Sociometric status.

Shall we,

Like crystal-gazing swami,

Evoke the Image

Of his Mommy?

Was he to Oedipus Complex fated

And Matriarchally Dominated,

Or forced,

By Rivalry with a Sibling,

To sucking his thumb, and forelock nibbling?

Was his Behavior Pattern derived

From being Culturally Deprived?
How did the Correlation worsen
'Twixt him and
The Total Mother Person?
And did he find no satisfaction
In Mother-Infant Interaction?
In what respect did his father fail
On the current Parental Acceptance Scale?

Perhaps on discipline Dad laid stress,
Instead of
Informed Permissiveness,
And spanked him when he kicked or bit
Or choked himself in a temper fit,

Instead of waiting to behold
Growth Process
Gradually
Unfold.
Perhaps he sentenced this child unlucky
To sleep without his Snuggle-Ducky,
And undermined his love of clan —
His Sibling Amicability Span.

Was he with siblings overstocked
By whom his every step was blocked?
His oldest brother,
Nickersnee,
Was twice as selfish as can be;
Then came his brother Nicolnursus,
Always cantankerous and versus.
Last,
Baby-sister Nicolette,
Her Daddy's joy,
Her Mommy's pet.
Poor Nicholas,
As he then was known,
Had nothing he could call his own;
He always ended in the middle —
Not first,
Not second,
Not *any* fiddle.
His brothers grabbed like octopuses
His slingshots and his abacuses;
They seized with bellows of "Skidoo!"
The blanket that he loved to chew.

He was unpunctual for meals
Because,
In spite of his appeals,
They gave to the community chest
The only timepiece he possessed —
A wrist sundial so unique
It only lost
Two days a week.
Yes, in a gesture truly generous
They gave away his primitive Benrus,
And left the future Santa Claus
Not ever knowing what time it was.
His little sister always ate
The choicest morsels off his plate
And wiped her mouth
Upon his sleeve
Without so much as "By your leave."
She snipped the buttons
Off his suit,
And Dad and Mommy thought it cute.

His favorite plaything,
Should she spot it,
She clamored for
Until she got it.
Each toy to which he got adjusted
His family borrowed,
Swiped,
Or busted.
He gazed around his room and blubbered —
'Twas bare as Mother Hubbard's cupboard.
In dark despair did he exist,
A thwarted young philanthropist
Who would have loved to give his toys
To underprivileged girls and boys,
But no one anywhere could he see
As underprivileged
As he.

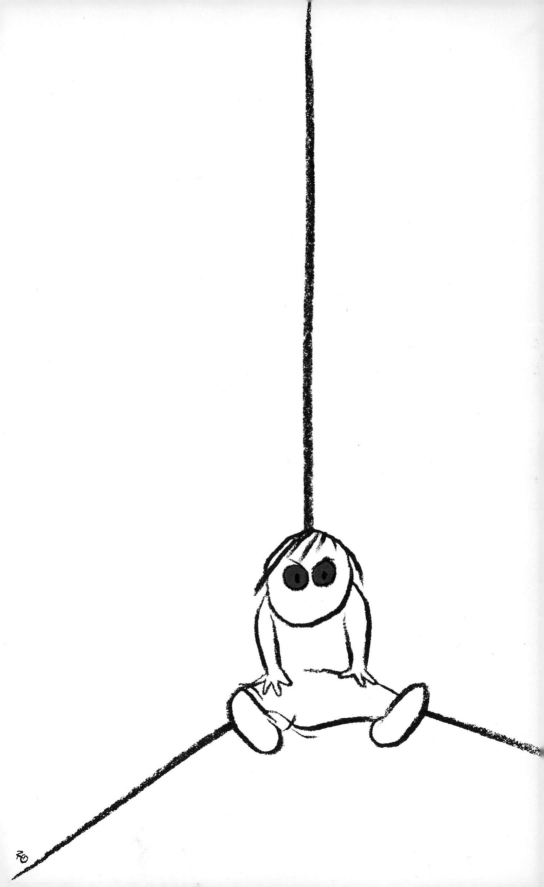

Here let us pause
To take a look
At Doctor William Sheldon's book
"Varieties of Human Physique."
It's very popular this week.
It says
Our outer shapes reveal
The inner urges that we feel.
It names,
In learned terms and skilled,
Three principal types of body build,
As different as giants are from dwarfs.
They're Endo-,
Meso-,
And Ectomorphs.
Throw Meso- and Ecto- out the window,
Our boy was obviously Endo-.
The Endomorph,
Upon inspection,

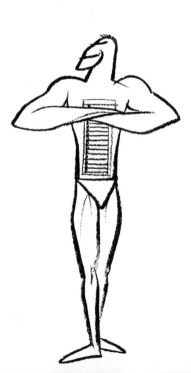

Is a glutton for food
And for affection.
He's sociable,
And loves his ease.
He has a strong desire to please.
He's soft and spherical in shape —
A little bit like a Concord grape.
He has an outsize stomach and liver
And is, I think,
A Compulsive Giver.

If thrown in water,
By the bye,
He sinketh not,
But floateth high.
I guess we needn't strain our wits
To guess who this description fits,
Who Doctor Sheldon had in mind
When Endomorphs
He first defined.
But if you want the answer quick,
I'll tell you who:
It was Saint Nick.
His nasty siblings eagerly noted
That he was spherical . . .
*And* he floated.

It made a jolly family scene
When they bobbed for him
On Halloween.
He didn't complain,
He didn't sulk,
He joined in laughter about his bulk.
One wish maintained his smile in bloom:
He liked to be liked,
No matter by whom,
And so he faced his tormenting family
With a smile perpetual and enamely.
But another wish was even stronger,
Was rooted deeper
And lasted longer:
An irresistible desire
That burned within him
Like a fire —
To win the name,
Through push or pull,
Of Lord
(Not Lady)
Bountiful.

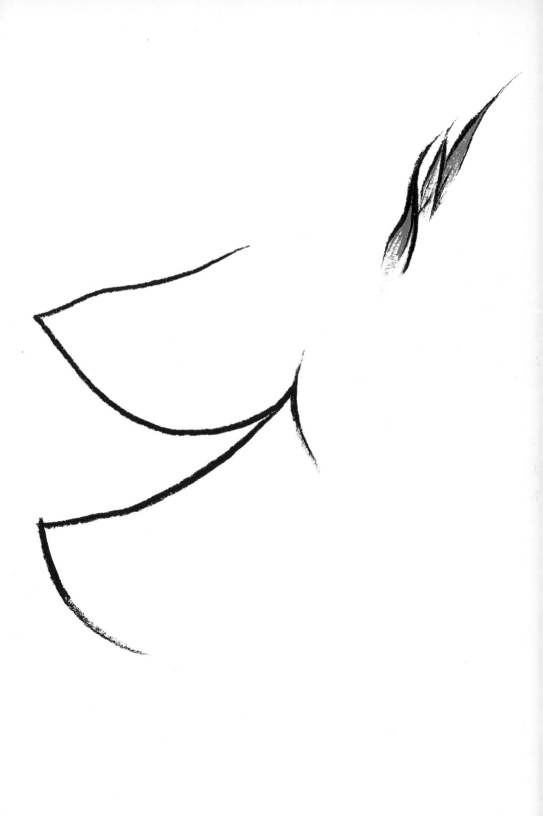

He was both hungering and thirsting
To have a storehouse simply bursting
With gifts,
And gifts,
And still more gifts,
Piled up like topless snowy drifts.
He didn't want to hoard this treasure;
To give it away
Would be his pleasure.
Then,
When his largess he had scattered,
He'd reach the only goal that mattered:
He'd be the source of joy and mirth,
The best-loved future saint on earth.

So —
Nick racked his brain and searched his soul.
How to attain
This golden goal?
He couldn't live
Another day
Unless he gave
*Something* away.
Yes, that was how he'd *have* to live.
But he didn't have a thing to give.
Now to himself this generous gnome
Said,
"Charity begins *from* home."
For several weeks
He disappeared,
Then turned up with a long white beard —
Perhaps the neatest of his tricks,
Considering he was only
Six.
He then cleaned out
With silent guile
His patriarchal domicile.

You couldn't call his pilfering petty —
He scattered presents
Like confetti.

He gave away his father's ox,
His ass,
His camel,
His hens and cocks,
His luscious figs,
His melons ripe,
His hubble-bubble hookah pipe,
His purple turban,
Or bandanna,
His milk,
His honey,
And his manna.

Ever his giving grew more reckless:
He gave away his mother's necklace,
Her veils all glittering with spangles,
Her beads,
Her baubles,

And her bangles,
Her slippers lined with cony fur,
Her nard,
Her frankincense and myrrh,
The skewers she used for shish kebab
And tasty Euphrates fish kebab.

He didn't shut his eyes when tempted,
And what he saw,
He soon pre-empted.
Among his brothers' things, he chose
Their knives, their arrows, and their bows,
Their shawms and psalters,
Flutes and zithers
(Which kept the tribe next door in dithers),

The chemicals they made bad smells with,
The cheetah that they chased gazelles with,
And, worst of all,
He gave away
Their comic books engraved on clay.
You may be sure he didn't forget
That little darling

Nicolette.
He gave away her music box,
Her nighties,
Pinafores,
And frocks,
Her silver mug,
Her fancy bib,
The lamp that glowed beside her crib,
Her orange-color porringer,
Her rattle
(Even oranger),
Her parasols,
Her folderols,
And even her papyrus dolls.

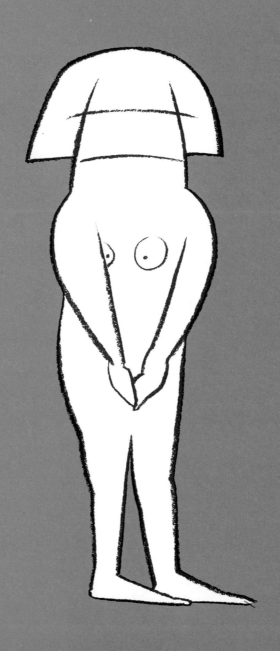

Next victims of his generous labors
Were unsuspecting friends and neighbors.
They mourned the loss of costly finery
With lamentations Asia Minory.
They used to sell their spice and gold
At profit of
A hundredfold;
But Nicholas had other plans
For the cargoes of their caravans,
And all their precious merchandise
Vanished
Before their very eyes —

Carried away,

As if by jinns,

To tents of wandering Bedouins.

Nick strewed their goods with lavish hand

All over sandy Nomad's Land,

Where all the children

And their mammas

Called him

The crocodile's pajamas.

But so did not

The victims of

His constant larcenous quest for love.

In fact,
They would have stoned or speared
This youngster with the snowy beard.
And that is why
This saint, or elf,
In order to fulfill himself,
Forsook his home in Asia Minor
In search of atmosphere benigner,
And either took a boat
Or swam
To Holland
And, later, New Amsterdam.
There,
Fleeing retroactive blame,
He discarded his baptismal name
And switched,
With hardly a moment's pause,
From Nicholas
To Santa Claus.

And Santa Claus he is today,
With his Ho-ho-ho!
And his Hey-hey-hey!
A simple joyous life he lives —
He just donates,
Bestows,
And gives.
Now, we,
As social scientists
And erudite child psychologists,
Have studied his youth
And clearly see
How preordained it was that he
Developed the only way he could —
From childhood
Into Robin Hood.
He isn't really morally blind;
Let's say he's only overkind.
'Twould be injustice to upbraid him
For being what
His psyche made him.

But do not swallow the story whole
Of that workshop
At the Arctic Pole,
And the legend of those tiny artisans,
His loyal tireless laboring partisans,
Covered with sawdust, grime, and pigments —
They're just imaginary figments.
When childish hearts at Christmas throb,
It's you and I who've done the job.
But when it comes
To claiming the credit,
Is Santa foremost?
You have said it!
Nothing could really be absurder
Than the way he gets away with murder.
I must admit we've helped him lots
With our tarradiddles to the tots,
But I'm tired now of his simper smug
As we sweep the truth beneath the rug.
Let us expose, and not applaud,
This smirking, sanctimonious fraud!

What shame and rage will he erupt to
When he knows we know what he's been up to!
He'll be laughing-stock of all the globe,
Hopes one ardent Santaclaustrophobe —
Yet I fear he is too sly by half,
And when Christmas bills pile up like chaff
He may have the final stocking-laugh.